# *The* Romans

First published in 1998 by Wayland Publishers Ltd,
61 Western Road, Hove, East Sussex BN3 1JD, England

Find Wayland on the Internet at
http://www.wayland.co.uk

**British Library Cataloguing in Publication Data**

Dargie, Richard
    The Romans in Scotland
    1. Romans – Scotland – Juvenile literature
    2. Rome – Civilization – Juvenile literature
    3. Scotland – History – to 1057 – Juvenile literature
    I. Title II. Hook, Richard
    936.1'1

ISBN 0 7502 2268 9

Editor: Carron Brown
Consultant: Donald Gunn, an Education Officer for
BBC Education Scotland
Designer: Joyce Chester
Production controller: Carol Titchener

Typeset in England by Joyce Chester
Printed and bound in Italy by G. Canale & C.S.p.A,
Turin

Cover pictures: Antonine's Wall; [inset] an iron Roman
mask found at Newstead Fort.
Endpapers: The Eildon Hills.
Contents page: Roman defences on Antonine's Wall at
Rough Castle. These pits contained sharp stakes at the
bottom that could kill any attacker that fell into them.

**Picture Acknowledgements**

C. M. Dixon 15; Sonia Halliday 22; Robert Harding
Picture Library *cover* [main], 11 (top); Dennis Hardley
*endpapers*; Historic Scotland/Crown copyright reserved,
Whithorn Priory, St. Peter Stone 37; National Museums
of Scotland 17, 18, 19, 26, 29, 30, 31, 34 (both), 35,
40 (top), 41; Scotland in Focus 4–5, 25, 32; Scottish
Trust For Underwater Archaeology/B. L. Andrian 11
(bottom); S T B/Still Moving *cover* [inset], 8, 16, 28, 35;
Vindolanda Trust 23 (bottom), 40 (bottom); Wayland
Picture Library 23 (top), 36, 38; David Williams 25.

Artwork supplied by: Peter Bull 9, 14, 24, 39; Kate
Davenport *cover* and chapter logo, 33; Richard Hook
6–7; 12–13, 20–21, 27; Sallie Alane Reason 43.

EvA
'Scd' History

# in Scotland

## Contents

# The Battle of Mons Graupius, AD 84

The first light of dawn crept across the barren moor. Battle trumpets sounded. Along the marshy plain at the bottom of the hillside, five lines of troops in leather tunics and bronze helmets edged into position. Each man drew his short sword and linked his shield with his neighbour's to form a solid metal wall. The Roman legion stood ready for battle.

On the hillside above, the enemy was waiting and preparing to attack. A loud roaring voice rang out. The Roman troops below did not understand the strange words but they knew the voice was taunting and insulting them. When the voice stopped, a flight of spears thudded into the Roman wall. Thirty chariots rumbled towards the Roman lines. The legionaries stood firm. They knew the chariots would be easily

beaten back by the legion's cavalry. After this first attack, the 5,000 legionaries of Rome prepared themselves to fight the hordes of tribal warriors who were yelling and charging down the hill.

The bloody struggle took several hours. The warriors were brave but no match for the well-armed, well-trained might of Rome. By noon, the tribal horde could take no more fighting. Throughout the afternoon, the Romans hunted down the surviving warriors, who had fled into the surrounding forests and marshes. By evening, the field was littered with dead. Only 360 of the corpses were Roman dead. But several thousand Caledonians of northern Britain lost their lives that day.

The Roman commander dined alone in his tent that evening and thought over the events of the day. The last enemies of Rome in the West had been defeated. The next morning he would send a letter to his Emperor to tell him that the Caledonians had been conquered.

# After the Battle

The commander rose early the next morning. While a slave prepared his breakfast, he stood at the door of his tent and looked out over the wild mountains of Caledonia. The commander was called Agricola. He was a fine soldier who had served the Roman Empire in Italy, Asia and Gaul. He had been Governor of Britannia for six years.

The Romans had invaded Britain in AD 43. Over the next forty years, they had gradually defeated all the tribes in the southern half of the island. By AD 78, when Agricola became Governor, only the tribes in the mountain areas of North Wales and Caledonia held out against the Romans. Agricola quickly conquered North Wales.

An iron Roman mask found at Newstead Fort.

He then built forts across northern England and prepared to invade Caledonia. In AD 80, his troops reached as far as the broad River Tay. The lands between the Forth and the Clyde were held by a chain of Roman forts. In AD 83, Agricola sent his fleets out to stir up trouble along the northern coasts. Now he had defeated the main Caledonian army in open battle.

Agricola expected the Celts to come down to his camp and surrender. He expected that, like all the other peoples of the Empire, they would give up their old warlike customs. In time, they would become peaceful citizens of Rome. Agricola ordered his officers to prepare for the surrender.

No tribesmen arrived that morning. The Caledonians had burnt their homes and farms and disappeared deep into the hills and glens of the north and west. There they could hide, rest and recover their strength. The summer was almost over. The Caledonians knew that the invader would have to feed his troops and horses through the long cold winter months. The Romans could not follow them into the wilderness without supplies. Agricola ordered his men to march back to the safety of his forts in the south.

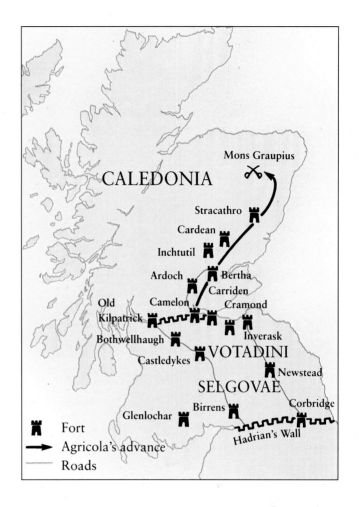

This map shows Agricola's route to Mons Graupius, and the Roman forts, roads and walls that were built during the time the Romans stayed in Scotland.

Within months, Agricola was ordered back to Rome. The next Roman commander to arrive in Britannia was afraid to risk losing men in a northern campaign. The Romans had won the battle of Mons Graupius but they had failed to defeat the Caledonian tribes. Caledonia would never be part of the Roman Empire.

# The Celtic Peoples of Caledonia

The Romans called the enemy Caledonians. These tribes were Celtic people. The Celtic homeland was in Austria in Central Europe. The Celts were a skilled people who discovered how to make weapons from iron. From 800 BC, they invaded northern Europe and the British Isles.

The Celts were farmers, traders and warriors. Some tribes lived in hill-forts. They built their houses around the peak of a hill and then built around the village. The strongest inner walls were made of stone blocks and the outer ramparts were made of heaped earth. To enter the hill-fort, you had to pass through high wooden gates. Some hill-forts, such as Eildon Hill near Melrose, were large enough to hold several thousand people.

Other Celtic families lived in brochs or in crannogs. Brochs were high, round towers. They each had a low, narrow entrance tunnel. There were no windows in the thick stone walls. Brochs were usually built near farmland and by the edge of the sea. We think that Celtic tribes used them as a place of safety when they were attacked. More than 500 of these strong ancient fortresses survive in Scotland today. Many brochs are found in northern counties such as Caithness and in the Orkney and Shetland Islands.

Some Celts built crannogs, or houses on water. Long wooden poles were driven down into the muddy bed of a loch. These were bound together to form a base on to which the house was built, slightly above the loch's surface. The wooden bridge linking the crannog to the shore could be cut in times of trouble.

Each Celtic house had a thatched roof and a timber frame. The walls were made of a woven frame of wicker or sticks. They were made windproof and waterproof by a covering of stretched animal skin or a type of plaster made from mud and straw.

Below: A reconstructed crannog house on Loch Tay in Perthshire.

Above: Many stone brochs still survive today in good condition. This example is at Rickisbrough in the Shetland Islands.

# Life in a Celtic House

We know a lot about the Celts and how they lived. Several Roman writers travelled in Celtic lands such as Gaul and Britannia. These Roman writers said that the Celts were tall people with reddish or fair hair. Celtic men grew 'moustaches so long that their mouths were covered up, their food got tangled and their drink was taken in, almost through a strainer.' Young Celtic warriors grew their hair long and were forbidden to cut it until they had killed an enemy in battle. Not all the Celts were fair haired, so some women dipped their hair in bowls of stale urine to lighten it. Celtic women also coloured their lips with the dark juice of fruits such as elderberry.

The Celts were skilled people and knew how to weave cloth from wool on a loom. They liked checked and patterned cloth. Men wore trousers called *bracae* or breeches. Women wore long gowns. All Celts liked to wear long flowing cloaks Rich Celts fastened their cloaks at the shoulder with a decorated metal brooch whilst the poor fastened their cloaks with sharp thorns taken from plants. The Celts wore leather shoes.

The Celts spoke their own languages but we know very little about them. No written records from the Celts have survived.

**This illustration shows a Celtic family at home inside a hill-fort.**

A rich Celtic tribe had many cattle, sheep, pigs and goats. Celtic tribes travelled long distances each spring taking their herds up to fresh summer pastures in the hills. In winter, cattle were led to village barns for shelter. The Celts lived in northern lands where the growing season was short. Their main crops were oats, barley and lentils. These were good crops for a cold, wet climate like Caledonia. The crops were harvested using a curved iron tool called a sickle. The Celts added to their diet by hunting and fishing. The great forests of Caledonia gave them venison, berries and mushrooms. The rivers gave them salmon, trout and shellfish. Forest plants gave them medicines and dyes for their cloth.

# The Roman World

The Romans were one of the great peoples of the ancient world. The city of Rome was the capital of an empire that stretched across Europe, Asia Minor and North Africa. The earliest Romans were an Iron Age tribe in central Italy. They built a fortress around seven hills which surrounded the River Tiber.

**This map shows the extent of the Roman Empire in AD 117.**

The Romans were clever at war. They had a powerful army led by skilful generals. They learnt how to navigate and they built a fleet of warships. They also knew how to build up their territory and power. They conquered neighbouring peoples, then offered them peace and the chance to become Roman citizens. In this way, they turned enemies into allies. By the year 30 BC, the Romans controlled all the lands around the Mediterranean Sea.

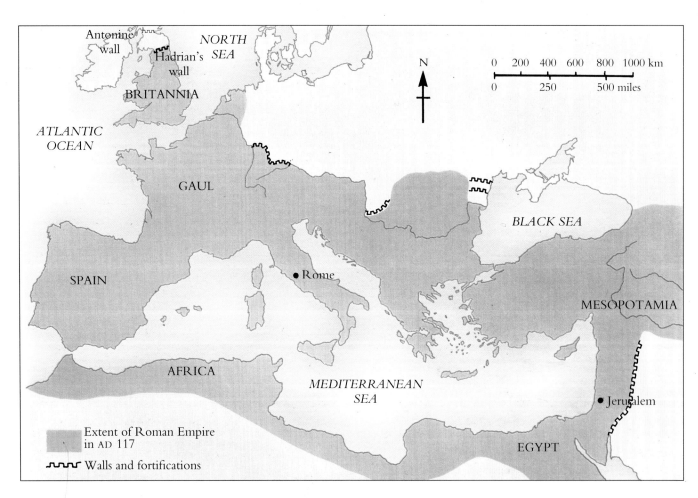

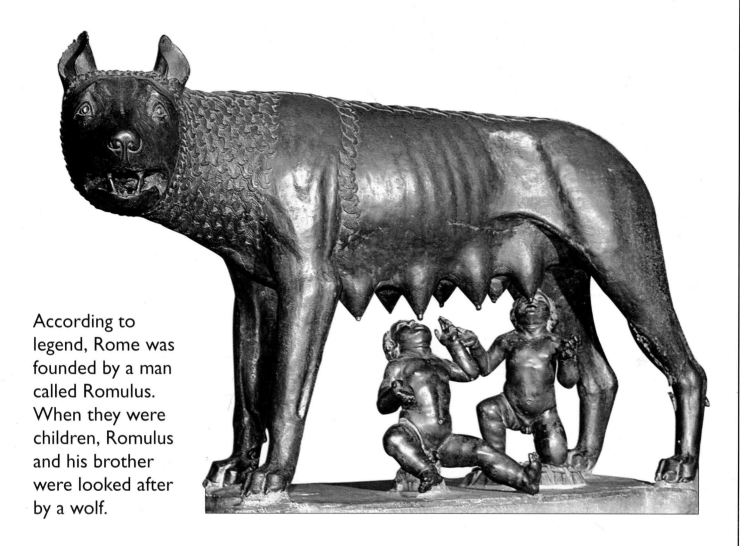

According to legend, Rome was founded by a man called Romulus. When they were children, Romulus and his brother were looked after by a wolf.

The peoples of the Roman Empire were united by a shared way of life. The language of the Empire was the Roman tongue of Latin. There was a common currency that bore the head of the Emperor. One set of Roman laws was used throughout the Empire. All the lands in the Empire were defended by the Roman legions.

The Romans liked to live in towns. They were also great builders and engineers. They founded new cities in all the lands that they conquered.

In every Roman city, they built temples to their gods. There was a large open market place called the forum where their merchants could meet. Most Roman towns had public baths where people could go to wash and meet their friends. Roman cities were supplied with fresh running water and had drains and sewers to take away refuse. All the towns and cities of the Empire were linked together by straight, well-made roads. These roads carried troops, goods and important messages across the Empire.

# The Conquest of Britannia

By the year 60 BC, the Romans had only one enemy left in Europe. This was the Celtic peoples. The Romans always feared the Celts.

A raiding Celtic army had invaded Italy and defeated Rome in 390 BC. The Romans believed the Celts were jealous of their rich southern lands.

This sculpture shows a Roman soldier on horseback killing Celts during a battle.

A carnyx or trumpet which the Celts used in battle. The picture above shows the head of a carnyx. The illustration on the right shows what a complete carnyx would have looked like.

The brilliant Roman general Julius Caesar defeated the Celtic kingdoms of Gaul in 58 BC. Caesar's troops twice landed in the south of Britannia and fought the British Celts. However, the German Celts were too strong for the Romans. Walls and forts were built along the German frontier to keep the Celtic 'barbarians' out of the Empire.

In AD 43, the Romans decided to invade Britain. They knew that the British Celts had been sending weapons and warriors to Celtic rebels in Gaul. The Romans believed that Britain was rich in valuable minerals such as gold, silver and tin. The new Roman Emperor Claudius wanted to fight and win a war against the Celts. This would make him popular with the Roman people.

Four Roman legions sailed from Gaul in AD 43. About 20,000 troops landed on the British south coast. Some southern chiefs surrendered to the Romans. They were allowed to keep their lands. Other tribes fought the invader but were forced back into their hill-forts. Twenty of these forts were captured and destroyed in the first summer of the invasion. However, it took many years for the Romans to conquer the fierce Welsh tribes. In the north of England, a warlike people called the Brigantes held out against the Romans. By AD 80, however, the Romans under Agricola had taken control of most of southern Britain. Now they could march north to deal with the Caledonians.

# The Invasion of Caledonia

Agricola's legions marched into northern Britain in the spring of AD 80. Some of the Celtic tribes, such as the Votadini of East Lothian, accepted Roman rule. Other tribes resisted. The Selgovae defended their fortress of Eildon Hill but it was soon captured. The inhabitants were slaughtered. A great camp for the legions was built nearby at Trimontium, now known as Newstead. Most of the tribes in southern Caledonia made peace with the powerful new invader.

Important Roman soldiers may have worn masks to frighten their enemies.

Agricola then explored the lands north of the River Tay. Major forts were built at Camelon near Falkirk, Castledykes on the Clyde and at Inchtuthil in Strathmore. A line of smaller forts was built to watch for the enemy's approach. Roads were built to link these forts together. The northern tribes were defeated at Mons Graupius. By the end of AD 84, it seemed that Caledonia would become Roman land.

Yet Agricola was soon called away from Britannia. Legions were taken from Britain to patrol other parts of the Empire. One legion was left in York with the job of policing all of eastern and northern Britain. The Caledonians saw that the Romans were weakened. One by one the forts built by Agricola were attacked and destroyed. By AD 100, the Romans had little to show for their efforts to conquer Caledonia.

Chamfrons were leather and iron-studded helmets for horses. They were used to protect the horses from injury in battle.

# The Mystery of the Ninth

The Ninth Legion was called the Hispana. The Ninth had 5,600 foot soldiers. Most of these men came from Pannonia in what is modern-day Hungary. The legion also had 800 auxiliaries or 'helpers'. These were native troops who fought on the Roman side. There were also a hundred cavalrymen in the legion. They scouted ahead on their horses when the legion was marching through dangerous territory.

This shows one of the legends surrounding the disappearance of the Ninth Legion. The Celts have attacked the Roman soldiers and captured the Ninth's eagle standard.

The Ninth Legion had crossed over to Britain in AD 43. They had defeated the tribes of northern England and built a fortress as their base at York. They had marched into Caledonia with Agricola. They had lost many men when the Caledonians launched a surprise night attack on their marching camp. Some of their troops were also sent to help fight the Celts in Germania. By AD 100, the Ninth Legion was seriously weakened.

Around the year AD 105, the Ninth Legion simply disappeared. Historians do not know what happened to it. One legend says that it was ordered to march north into Caledonia to put down a rebellion. It was never heard of again. Some writers think that the Caledonians lured the legion into a trap and slaughtered it. This massacre is said to have happened on the Solway Firth near the present-day border with England. Some officers who escaped were punished for the disgrace of losing the Ninth's precious eagle standard to the Celts.

Archaeologists have studied the rubbish pits and toilet heaps left at the forts where the Ninth Legion was based. We know that nothing much was added to these pits between the years AD 108 and 125. This tells us that the forts had probably been abandoned by the legion. Either the legion was destroyed by the Celts or it was moved to another part of the Empire.

# Hadrian's Wall

In AD 117, Hadrian became Emperor of Rome. He believed that the Empire was too large for the army to defend properly. He wanted to make the frontiers safer. In AD 120, there was a rebellion in northern Britain. Hadrian decided that he could not afford to waste money on trying to keep Caledonia peaceful. He decided to build a wall from the River Tyne to the Solway Firth. Here Britain was only 117 km wide.

Roman engineers chose the ground so that the wall was always on high ground. In places, the wall was 5 m high and 3 m wide. Most of it was built of stone. At the western end, timber and turf were used instead.

Only the stone foundations of Hadrian's Wall survive today. The wall was much higher in Roman times. This section near Housesteads Fort uses the local cliffs to make it more difficult to attack.

On the Caledonian side, the Romans dug a steep ditch. This would slow down any attackers. On the southern side of the wall, there was a second ditch called the *vallum*. This marked off the military zone around the wall. Even peaceful Britons were not allowed to enter this area.

Sixteen large forts were built along the wall. Each fort was the home for about 1,000 soldiers. There were smaller forts called milecastles. These were built 1,460 m apart. This distance was a Roman mile. Each milecastle held about thirty men. Between the milecastles, there were watch-towers.

Hadrian originally came from Spain. He was one of the most powerful Roman Emperors.

From these, the Roman sentries could watch the roads that led towards the wall. Hadrian's Wall was a network of watch-towers, forts and army camps. More than 15,000 Roman troops were based in the wall zone. They could flash signals along the wall to tell commanders if there was trouble. The roads through the wall were strictly controlled. It would be harder for the Celtic tribes to plot together against the Romans. Hadrian also built the wall to impress the Celts with the might of Rome. He wanted to show that the border of the Roman Empire in Britain was now fixed for all time.

A Roman milecastle fort has been reconstructed at Vindolanda. This shows the parapet and main gate.

# Antonine's Wall

The Romans made one more attempt to conquer Caledonia. In AD 141, Emperor Antonine ordered the legions to march north once more. He then ordered them to build a second wall across Britain. This one stretched across Caledonia from the Forth to the Clyde. Antonine's Wall was almost 60 km long. It had forts every 3 km. The wall was made of turf blocks laid on a stone foundation. Along the top of the wall, the Romans built a palisade. This was a tough wall of sharp, pointed wooden stakes.

Antonine's Wall was over 6 m high. Behind the wall ran a military road, so that troops could move quickly to any point of danger on the wall. On the banks of the rivers Forth and Clyde, the Romans built watch-towers in case the Caledonians tried to slip across. There were regular beacon platforms which could be lit in an emergency. Milestones were placed along the length of the wall.

**This diagram shows the forts that were built along Antonine's Wall.**

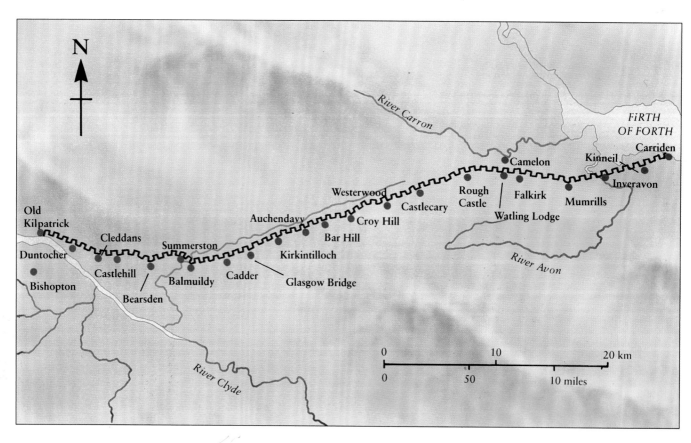

This milestone, found near Glasgow, bears the name ANT NINO or Antonine, the emperor who built the second northern wall.

We know the name of the commander who carried out Emperor Antonine's instructions to build a wall across Caledonia. The name Lollius Urbicus is carved on a stone tablet that was found at Balmuildy near Glasgow. Lollius was the Roman general in charge of the Twentieth Legion who planned and built most of the second wall.

This second wall across northern Britain had an important purpose. The peaceful tribes of southern Caledonia, such as the Votadini, were now under Roman protection. The Romans could also keep a close watch on the dangerous tribes in the far north. The Romans manned the wall for the next thirty years. After that, they decided to retreat to the southern wall built by the Emperor Hadrian. Later Roman emperors, such as Severus, sent legions northwards into Caledonia but they were never able to control the Celts for long.

# A Legionary on Duty

The legionaries who patrolled southern Caledonia were well equipped. Their body armour was made of overlapping strips of metal which were buckled together by strips of leather. The armour was strong but moved easily. Under it they wore woollen tunics. Their helmets were made of bronze and leather.

Legionaries wore leather sandals. The soles were strengthened by hobnails to make them last. Caledonia was cold so most soldiers wore thick woollen cloaks. Archaeologists recently found a letter from a mother to her son who was serving on Hadrian's Wall. She had sent him woollen socks and underpants to help him keep warm.

This sculpture shows three Roman soldiers carrying the *scutum* or shield and the *pilum* or spear.

The legionaries had to keep their fort in good order. Every day they repaired timbers on the palisade and cleared bushes away from the ditch. They also had to check on the food and weapon supplies in their fort. The officer in charge of the fort was the centurion. He had to send reports to his commander. These were written on writing tablets made of wood and covered in wax. The report was etched on the wax using a pointed iron nib called a stylus.

Regular parades were held in the largest forts. Officers wore a special parade uniform which was more decorative than their battle dress. They also wore ornamental parade masks made of bronze. After parade, the troops spent the day at their tasks such as training horses for the cavalry or cleaning weapons. The blacksmith's forge and the armoury were busy places in a large fort. Some troops worked in the bakehouse preparing food for the legion. At the end of the day, the soldiers went to the bath house. Here the men could relax in the steam room and thaw out after a day in the cold Caledonian climate.

**A Roman legionary looked like this. He wore body armour and a helmet and carried a shield, spear and sword.**

# A Frontier at Peace

The Romans patrolled the northern frontier for over 300 years. There were short periods of war. Most of the time, however, the border with Caledonia was at peace. Roman troops were always on watch, controlling the roads and looking for any signs of unrest. Very little fighting took place along the two great walls of Hadrian and Antonine.

We know that the Celts mixed with the Romans. Many Celts picked up Roman ways of life such as speaking Latin and wearing togas or Roman cloaks. Roman goods and coins have been found at Celtic village sites. At the hilltop fortress of Traprain Law in East Lothian, a great treasure of Roman silver goblets and plates has been found. We think that this was a gift from a local Roman commander to the chief of a friendly tribe.

This bronze helmet was found in Scotland. We think it was used by a cavalryman for parades. This is the back of the helmet.

This treasure hoard of Roman silver goblets and plates was found at Traprain Law in East Lothian.

The first legionaries in Caledonia were originally Roman citizens. Often these men married local Celtic women from friendly tribes such as the Votadini. Their sons were half-Roman, half-Celtic. In turn, they joined their father's regiment. At first, they acted as scouts, moving amongst the Celts looking for signs of trouble. By AD 200, legionaries were recruited from the local population.

There were market places across southern Caledonia, called *loca*, where the Romans and Celts could trade. One was called *Taba* or Tay. Another called Daunoni was on the Clyde west of Antonine's Wall. Roman merchants bought Caledonian goods and shipped them to Europe. The main goods were leather hides, timber and wool. We know of one very unusual Caledonian export. A large bear was caught in the Highlands and taken to Rome in AD 80. It was slaughtered by gladiators on the opening day of the Colosseum amphitheatre.

# Daily Life on the Frontier

Small villages soon grew up around the forts on Antonine's Wall. Traders lived here, selling goods to the legionaries. Many Celtic tribes moved near to the wall so that they could be protected from other tribes by the legion. They set up farms selling meat and other foods to the centurions in charge of the legion's granaries. At Bearsden, there was even a pottery kiln where one local merchant called Sarrius made pots, jugs and plates to sell to the legion.

It was common for legionaries to settle near the wall when their twenty-five years of service were over. Many married local Caledonian women. They became farmers or opened small shops and tried to live by their skills as craftsmen. Many of these men were born in the frontier area. It made sense to them to retire in the only part of the vast Roman Empire where they felt at home. Here they could settle and raise a family in peace.

Coarse pottery like this was used by the Romans for everyday use. Some of these pots were made in Britain, others were shipped in from other parts of the Empire.

Many farming and craft tools have been found in areas near to Roman forts. Iron scythe blades have been found at Bar Hill and Loudoun hill-forts. Iron rakes, and also one made of deer antler, are another sign that crops were grown on these farms which sheltered behind the Roman wall. Many other kinds of metal tool have also been discovered. These important finds tell us that the Romans brought their skills as carpenters, stonemasons, blacksmiths and wheelwrights to southern Caledonia.

**These farming tools are almost 2,000 years old and were used by Roman and Celtic farmers in southern Scotland.**

The land between Hadrian's and Antonine's Wall slowly became prosperous. There were over 16,000 soldiers living in the area. Each man was well paid by the Imperial Treasury in Rome. They had wages to spend in the shops and inns of the small towns and at hill-fort markets. Altogether, the army spent millions of *denarii* in the area each year.

# Building a Roman Road

The Romans built roads to link their forts together. Their roads were straight so troops could get from one place to another quickly. There were two main roads into Caledonia. The eastern route, called Dere Street, linked with Antonine's Wall near the fort at Camelon. A western road to the River Clyde followed the same route as the modern M74 from England to Glasgow.

Roman roads were as straight as possible so that the legions could travel quickly. This is Dere Street which crosses the Cheviot Hills.

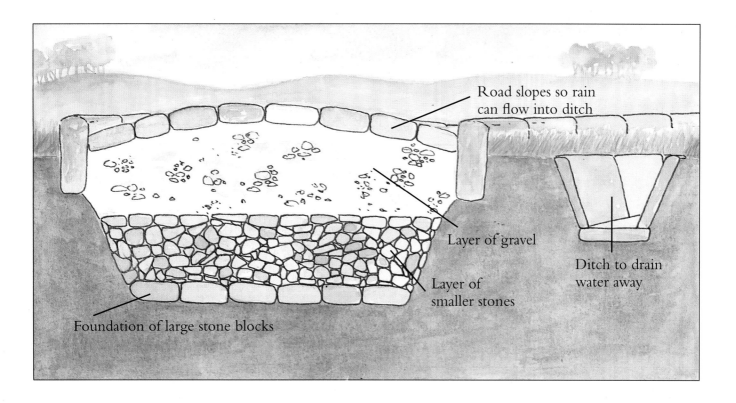

Road slopes so rain can flow into ditch

Layer of gravel

Ditch to drain water away

Layer of smaller stones

Foundation of large stone blocks

**This diagram shows a cross-section of a Roman road.**

Roman roads were 5 m wide. They had a foundation of stone blocks with top layers of smaller stones and gravel. The top of the road had a slope so that rain could drain to the side. Ditches carried the water away. All trees and bushes near the route of the road were cut down. This was to make sure travellers could not be ambushed. The Romans also built milestones so that travellers could tell how far they had gone. In peacetime, the roads were usually built by gangs of slaves. In wartime, the legionaries themselves might be employed as builders if a new road was needed quickly.

Most travellers on these roads moved by foot or on horseback. The Celts used chariots, but there is no evidence that the Romans used them in northern Britain. They did use wagons. These were covered carts pulled by teams of oxen. Pieces of ox harness and several Roman cart wheels have been found by archaeologists. The hub and spokes were made of wood but the wheel was strengthened by an iron tyre. These wagons were used for carrying supplies of grain to the soldiers in outlying forts. The Romans sometimes used small flat-bottomed cargo boats on the River Tweed to move goods. A steering oar for one of these boats has been discovered in a nearby fort.

# Roman and Celtic Gods

The Romans believed in many gods. Jupiter was the king of the gods. Venus was the goddess of love. Legionaries often made sacrifices to Mars, the god of war. Minerva was the goddess of wisdom and was said to look after the engineers in the army. After AD 200, many soldiers began to worship an eastern sun god called Mithras. A temple to Mithras has been discovered at Carrawburgh on Hadrian's Wall.

Below: The Romans cremated their dead and kept the ashes in special urns.

Right: This sculpture shows an animal sacrifice to the gods.

Roman sacrificial altars have been found in southern Scotland. These are stone pillars with carved inscriptions to a particular god such as Apollo. Soldiers used these altars to offer up animal sacrifices to their favourite gods. Many of these altars have been found along Antonine's Wall. Roman legions usually cremated their dead.

The Celts believed in spirits and gods. There were special holy times of the year which marked the changing seasons. Beltane, the first day in May, was celebrated with huge bonfires in honour of the god Belenos. Each tribe had its own rituals and ceremonies. Some tribes had a special sanctuary or grove in the forest. There they built wooden idols of their gods. Some Roman writers said that these idols were decorated with the severed heads of their enemies.

Most Celtic tribes believed in a life after death. They usually put food into the graves of their dead. Some Celtic chiefs were buried in their chariot. Other Celtic tribes often drowned or hanged their slaves as a sacrifice to the gods. When the Romans took over an area of Britannia, they allowed the Celts to worship their own gods. However, the Romans stamped out ceremonies based on human sacrifice.

At first the religions of the Romans and the Celts were very different. In time, they began to respect and worship each other's gods.

Brigantia, a Celtic goddess who was later worshipped by Roman legionaries.

35

# The Coming of the Cross

The Caledonian tribes and the Roman legionaries were pagans and worshipped many gods. However, a new religion began to spread across the Roman Empire. This was Christianity. Its believers followed the teachings of a man in the Middle East called Jesus Christ. He was crucified in Jerusalem in AD 30. His followers believed that he had come to life again soon after and had left to live in heaven.

**A Christian being eaten alive by a lion in an arena in Rome.**

The Christian message was very powerful. Christian groups called churches sprung up in every part of the Empire. There were some Christians in Britannia by the early second century. But some Roman emperors were suspicious of the Christians and punished them or made them into slaves. In Rome, some Christians were taken to the Colosseum and tortured for the amusement of the crowd. In Britannia, Christians often hid in forests and caves. They had to meet and worship in secret.

In AD 312, Constantine became Roman Emperor. He believed that Jesus Christ had helped him to defeat his enemies. Christianity became the official religion of the Empire. By AD 330, there were many Christians amongst the legionaries and the Caledonian tribes. By AD 400, we know there were even Christian kingdoms in Caledonia. The pagan Votadini now lived in the Christian kingdom of Gododdin.

The earliest Christian leader in Caledonia was probably a missionary called Ninian. We think he was the son of a Roman soldier who served on Hadrian's Wall. As a young man, he studied the Bible at monasteries in Rome and in Gaul. In AD 397, he was made a bishop and sent to spread the Gospel in Caledonia. He travelled to Galloway in south-west Scotland. He was soon joined by a band of devoted followers. Ninian and his friends travelled throughout southern Caledonia and converted several Celtic tribes to the teachings of Christ.

**This early Christian cross is from Whithorn in Galloway. Ninian and his followers built a small stone church there. It was probably the first Christian church in Scotland.**

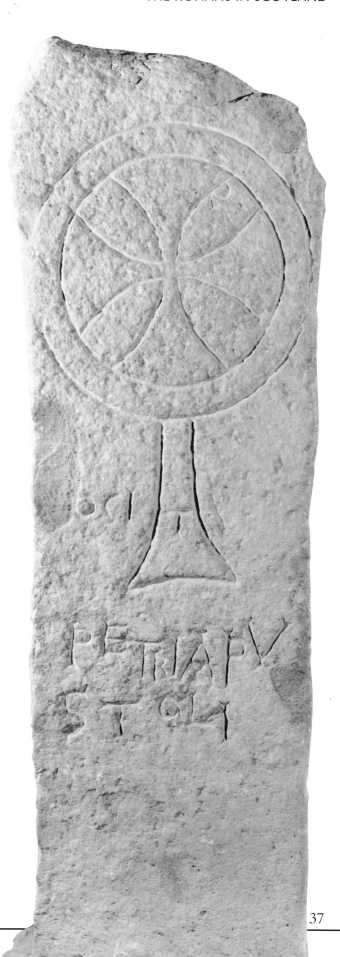

# The Fate of the Legions

After AD 250, new enemies began to threaten Britannia. A powerful Gaelic-speaking tribe from Ireland, called the Scots, began to raid the western coasts. New barbarians, the Angles, Saxons and Jutes, sailed from Germania and attacked the eastern shores. The Romans had to build forts and watch-towers around the whole area. Towns in every part of Britannia had to build strong, high walls to defend themselves from these raiders.

There was also a new enemy in the north. The Caledonian tribes had united into one nation called the Picts. The Pictish armies were strong enough to raid deep into the southern half of the island. Hadrian's Wall was no barrier to these northern warriors.

After AD 300, most Roman settlements in Britain needed stronger defences. The late Roman fort at Portchester would have looked like this.

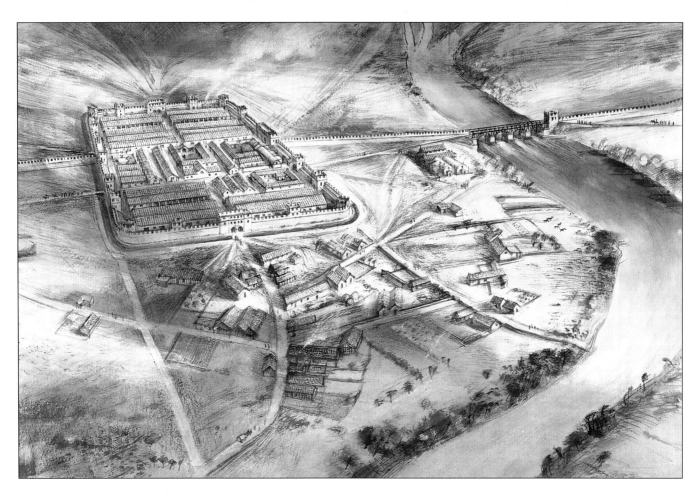

In AD 367, an alliance of the Caledonian Picts, Scots from Ireland and German Celts destroyed the Roman legions in Britannia. The Empire had to send fresh troops from other areas to restore order to the province.

The Romans also had to face new dangerous enemies in Europe. Barbarian peoples were pressing against the Empire. One of these, the Goths, defeated a huge Roman army and killed the Emperor. The rich provinces of Gaul, Spain and Italy were defenceless. In AD 410, the Goths took over the city of Rome itself. The Romans needed every soldier to defend the heart of their Empire.

In that year, all Roman troops in Britain were transferred to Gaul. The forts along the Caledonian frontier were abandoned for ever. The peaceful people of Britannia were told that they would have to defend themselves. One British writer who lived at this time wrote 'the barbarians drive us into the sea. The sea drives us to the barbarians. Between these two kinds of death, we are to be slaughtered or drowned.' The long years of the Roman peace were over.

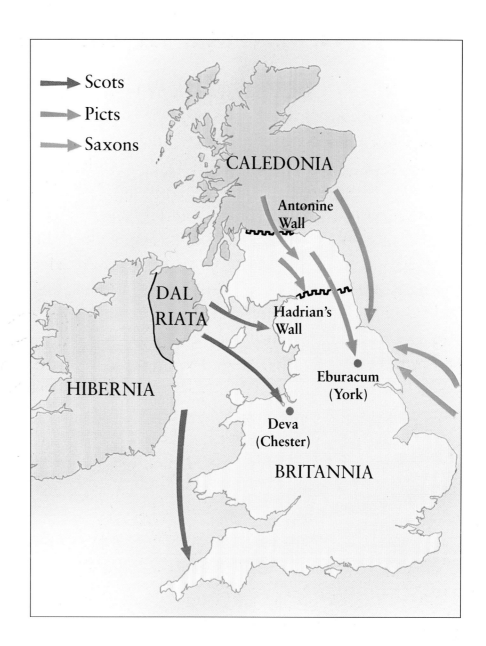

This map shows how the Picts, Scots and Celts began to attack the Romans in Britannia.

# How Do We Know About the Romans in Scotland?

In the last hundred years, archaeologists have discovered many Roman objects at digs across southern Scotland. Scotland has some of the best-preserved Roman defences to be found anywhere in Europe. Thanks to these studies we know a great deal about how the Romans built forts, camps and roads.

The soil of southern Scotland is often soft and full of peat. This has helped to preserve some objects for almost 2,000 years. Several pairs of leather Roman shoes have been found at Newstead Fort. Even pieces of Roman cloth and some checked Celtic plaid have survived.

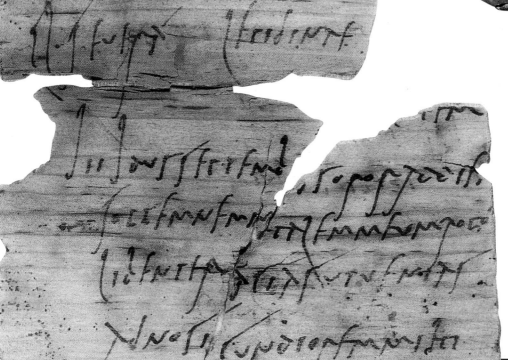

Above: Examples of well-preserved Roman shoes – last worn 2,000 years ago.

Left: An invitation to a Roman birthday party written in ink on a wooden writing tablet.

Roman rubbish dumps have been examined. Broken glass and tiles tell us that Roman buildings in Scotland were dry and windproof. Bones and other pieces of food refuse tell us what the Romans ate. At the fort of Vindolanda on Hadrian's Wall, hundreds of pieces of letters have survived in a rubbish pit. These fragments tell us a great deal about the daily lives of ordinary soldiers on the Caledonian frontier.

Sometimes archaeologists find things that were deliberately hidden by ancient people. Probably this was done in times of trouble. Workers in Falkirk were levelling a building site when they found an old pot stopped with plaid cloth. It contained a treasure of almost 2,000 Roman silver pennies. Many of these coins were minted long after the Romans abandoned Antonine's Wall. This tells us that the Caledonians still traded with the Roman province of Britannia to the south.

A Roman treasure hoard of silver pennies – buried for safety and then forgotten.

# Glossary

**Allies**  Friendly people who fought on the Roman side.

**Asia Minor**  The Roman name for modern-day Turkey.

**Barbarians**  The Roman name for tribes like the Celts and Germans who lived outside the Roman Empire.

**Beacon platforms**  Wooden towers with fires in metal containers. The fires were used for signalling danger along Roman walls.

**Caledonia**  The Roman name for Scotland north of the River Forth. Sometimes used for all of Scotland.

**Cavalry**  Soldiers mounted on horseback.

**Chariots**  Wheeled carts used in warfare and for ceremonies by the Romans and the Celts.

*Denarii*  A Roman coin of small value. The forerunner of the British penny.

**Eagle standard**  An eagle-topped pole that carried the battle honours of a Roman Legion.

**Fleets**  The warships of the Roman Empire.

**Foundation**  The base level of a building or a structure.

**Frontier**  Borderlands.

**Gaul**  The Roman name for modern-day France.

**Gospel**  The Christian message described in the first four books of the New Testament.

**Granaries**  Storehouses where grain and other food supplies were kept.

**Hobnails**  Metal studs hammered into a leather boot sole to make the sole wear down more slowly.

**Iron Age**  The period after 1000 BC when early peoples discovered how to make tools and weapons from iron ore.

**Legion**  A regiment in the Roman army of between 5,000 and 6,000 men.

**Legionaries**  The ordinary soldiers in a Legion.

**Navigate**  To sail a ship by a known, fixed course.

**Ramparts**  Defensive walls of heaped earth, often topped with a wooden wall of sharpened poles.

**Roman Empire**  The territories conquered and ruled by the Romans in Europe, Asia and North Africa.

**Scouts**  Troops sent ahead of the main army to look for signs of the enemy.

**Shellfish**  Shelled seafood such as mussels.

**Turf blocks**  Squares of grass turf piled on each other to make a wall that was thick and could not be set on fire.

**Venison**  The meat from wild deer.

**Watch-towers**  Wooden towers built along Roman walls so that soldiers could keep a look at for enemies.

**Wheelwrights**  Skilled craftsmen who made wheels for chariots and carts.

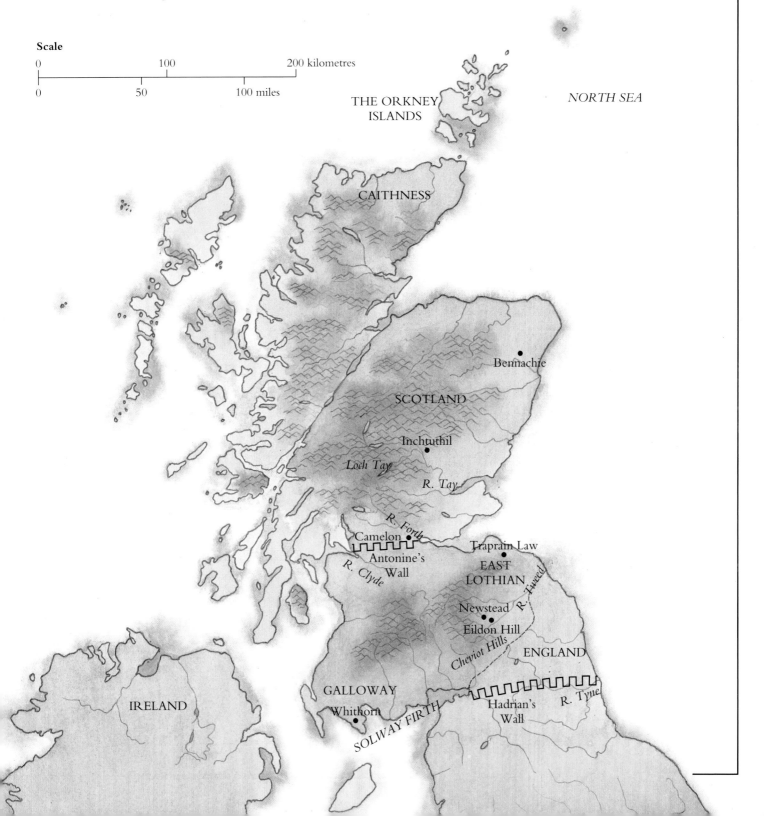

# Map of Scotland

including places mentioned in the text

THE SHETLAND
ISLANDS

**Scale**

| 0 | | 100 | | 200 kilometres |
| 0 | 50 | | 100 miles | |

THE ORKNEY
ISLANDS

*NORTH SEA*

CAITHNESS

SCOTLAND

Bennachie

Inchtuthil

*Loch Tay*

*R. Tay*

*R. Forth*

Camelon

Antonine's
Wall

*R. Clyde*

Traprain Law

EAST
LOTHIAN

*R. Tweed*

Newstead

Eildon Hill

*Cheviot Hills*

ENGLAND

GALLOWAY

IRELAND

Whithorn

Hadrian's
Wall

*R. Tyne*

*SOLWAY FIRTH*

# Further Information

## Books to Read

For pupils:
*A History of Scotland Book One* by W. Moffat (Oxford University Press, 1984)
*The Best of Hadrian's Wall* by R. Birley, Roman Army Museum (Greenhead, 1995)
*The Romans* by Peter Hicks (Wayland, 1993)
*The Roman Wall Illustrated* by R. Embleton & F. Graham (F. Graham, 1992)
*What Do We Know About the Romans?* by Mike Corbishley (Simon & Schuster, 1991)

For teachers:
*Roman Scotland* by David J. Breeze (Historic Scotland & Batsford, 1996)
*The Agricola and the Germania* by Cornelius Tacitus (Penguin Classics, 1992)

## BBC Information

BBC Education Scotland has produced a range of resources on the Romans.

For radio – *The Romans*, a three-part unit of drama role-play programmes in
 *Scottish Resources 7–9* (transmission Spring 1998; available on cassette).
For TV – *The Romans in Scotland*, a five-part drama/documentary in
 *See You, See Me*; for 7–9 year olds (transmission Autumn 1996).
Poster pack – *Caledonians and Romans* is an A1-sized full colour poster
 accompanied by pupil activity material for 7–9 year olds.

Information on programmes and on ordering radio cassettes or print support
materials is available from:
BBC Education, Room 305,
5 Queen Street, Edinburgh EH2 1JF
Tel: 0131 248 4261

# Index